Women & Cats

Women & Cats

WOMEN & CATS WILL DO AS THEY PLEASE, AND
MEN AND DOGS SHOULD RELAX AND GET USED TO THE IDEA.

Editor/Design: Andrea Donner

Printed in Canada

© BIOS / Klein/Hubert / Peter Arnold, Inc.

STRONG

Never be bullied into silence.
Never allow yourself to be made a victim.
Accept no one's definition of your life,
but define yourself.

Harvey Fienstein

Always remember, there is more strength in you than you ever realized or even imagined. Certainly nothing can keep you down if you are determined to get on top of things and stay there.

Norman Vincent Peale

I'm not going to lie down and let trouble walk over me.

Ellen Glasgow

It is sometimes the most fragile things that have the power to endure and become sources of strength.

May Sarton

Nothing is so strong as gentleness, and nothing is so gentle as true strength.

Ralph Sockman

Strength does not come from physical capacity. It comes from an indomitable will.

Mahatma Gandhi

With the new day comes new strength and new thoughts.

Eleanor Roosevelt

CARING

Caring about others, running the risk of feeling, and leaving an impact on people brings happiness.

Rabbi Harold Kushner

© Norvia Behling

The greatest gift we can give one another is rapt attention to one another's existence.

Sue Atchley Ebaugh

A loving heart is the truest wisdom.

Charles Dickens

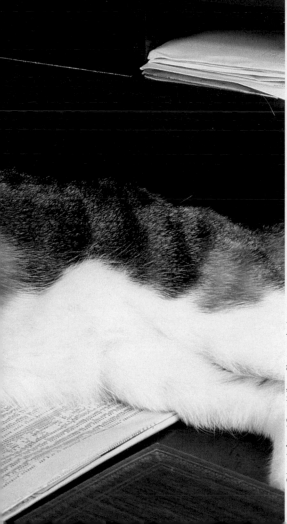

What the world really needs is more love and less paperwork.

Pearl Bailey

© Norvia Behling

FRIENDSHIP

To have a friend is one of the highest delights in life; to be a good friend is one of the noblest and most difficult undertakings.

Anonymous

If we would build on a sure foundation in friendship, we must love friends for their sake rather than for our own.

Charlotte Bronte

*The best things
in life are
never rationed.
Friendship,
loyalty, love,
do not require
coupons.*

G.T. Hewitt

The best kind of friend is the kind you can sit on a porch swing with, never say a word, then walk away feeling like it was the best conversation that you ever had.

Anonymous

Our perfect companions never have fewer than four feet.

Colette

© Frank Balthis

Each friend represents a world in us, a world not born until they arrive, and it is only by this meeting that a new world is born.

Anais Nin

To the world you might be one person, but to one person you might be the world.

Unknown

SELF-LOVE

Friendship with oneself is all important, because without it one cannot be friends with anyone else in the world.

Eleanor Roosevelt

© Aneal Vohra / Unicorn Stock Photos

I don't need anyone to rectify my existence. The most profound relationship we will ever have is the one with ourselves.

Shirley Maclaine

Partake of some of life's sweet pleasures.
And yes, get comfortable with yourself.

Oprah Winfrey

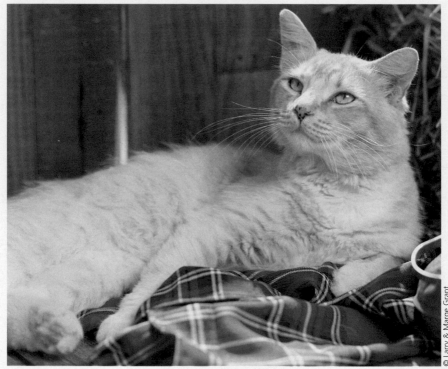

© Larry & Marge Grant

To love oneself is the beginning of a life long romance.

Oscar Wilde

© Cheryl Ertelt

*Self-love is the only weight-loss aid that
really works in the long run.*

Jenny Craig

One cannot think well, love well, sleep well,
if one has not dined well.

Virginia Woolf

A strong, positive self-image is the best possible preparation for success.

Dr. Joyce Brothers

© Alan & Sandy Carey

No quality is more attractive than poise — that deep sense of being at ease with yourself and the world.

Since you are like no other being ever created since the beginning of time, you are incomparable.

Brenda Ueland

© Frank Balthis

BEAUTIFUL

There is only one you for all time.
Fearlessly be yourself.

Anonymous

The best and most beautiful things in the world cannot be seen or even touched. They must be felt with the heart.

Helen Keller

*The kind of beauty I want
most is the hard-to-get kind
that comes from within —
strength, courage, dignity.*

Ruby Dee

It's beauty that captures your attention; personality which captures your heart.

Anonymous

INDEPENDENT

*Your vision will become clear only
when you look into your heart.
Who looks outside, dreams.
Who looks inside, awakens.*

If you always do what interests you,
at least one person is pleased.

Katharine Hepburn

Think like a queen. A queen is not afraid to fail.
Failure is another stepping stone to greatness.

Oprah Winfrey

You will make a lousy anybody else, but you will be the best "you" in existence.

Zig Ziglar

*No one can transcend
their own individuality.*

Arthur Schopenhauer

CONFIDENCE

Self-confidence is so relaxing. There is no strain or stress when one is self confident. Our lack of self-confidence comes from trying to be someone we aren't.

Anne Wilson Schaef

Life for both sexes is arduous, difficult, a perpetual struggle.
More than anything... it calls for confidence in oneself.

Virginia Woolf

In the middle of a world that has always been a bit mad,
the cat walks with confidence.

Roseanne Anderson

One of the things I learned the hard way was that it doesn't pay to get discouraged.

Lucille Ball

*Within your heart, keep one still, secret spot
where dreams may go.*

Louise Driscoll

© Sharon Eide & Elizabeth Flynn

DARING

*And the day came when the risk
to remain tight in a bud was
more painful than the risk
it took to blossom.*

Anais Nin

© Jane Burton / Bruce Coleman, Inc.

Bloom where you're planted.

Mary Engelbreit

All my life I have gone out on a limb, but I have turned the limb into a bridge, and there is cool, clear water flowing under.

Holly Near

Cats do not go for a walk to get somewhere, but to explore.

Sidney Denham

*Do not be too timid and squeamish...
All life is an experiment. The more
experiments you make, the better.*

Ralph Waldo Emerson

INTELLIGENT

*I happen to feel that the degree
of a person's intelligence is
directly reflected by the number
of conflicting attitudes
she can bring to
bear on the same topic.*

Lisa Alther

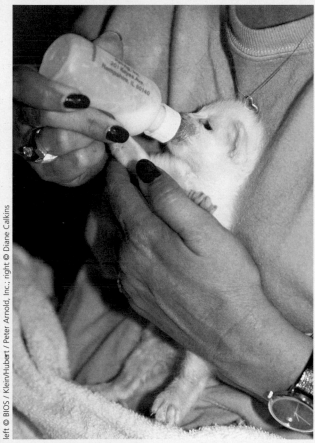

A woman uses her intelligence to find reasons to support her intuition.

Gilbert K. Chesterton

*There is no greater evidence
of superior intelligence than to be
surprised at nothing.*

Josh Billings

© Reed/Williams / Animals Animals

FUNNY

In this world, a good time to laugh is any time you can.

Linda Ellerbee

Taking joy in life is a woman's best cosmetic.

Rosalind Russell

Never be afraid to laugh at yourself. After all, you could be missing out on the joke of the century.

Dame Edna Everage

We cannot really love anybody with whom we never laugh.

Agnes Repplier

Humor is a wonderful way to prevent a hardening of the attitudes.

Joel Goodman

WISE

Happiness consists not in having,
but of being, not of possessing,
but of enjoying. It is the warm glow
of a heart at peace with itself.

Norman Vincent Peale

© Norvia Behling

*Women need real moments of solitude and self-reflection
to balance out how much of ourselves we give away.*

Barbara De Angelis

What a lovely surprise to discover how unlonely being alone can be.

Ellen Burstyn

One thing is certain, and I have always known it, the joys of my life have nothing to do with age.

May Sarton

Nobody really cares if you are miserable,
so you might as well be happy.

Cynthia Nelms

We can't take any credit for our talents. It's how we use them that counts.

Madeleine L'engle

© Rolf Kopfle

Accept everything about yourself – I mean everything.
You are you and that is the beginning and
the end – no apologies, no regrets.

Clark Moustakas